Life As ...

Life As a Native American on the Trail of Tears

Ann Byers

Cavendish Square

New York

Published in 2017 by Cavendish Square Publishing, LLC
243 5th Avenue, Suite 136, New York, NY 10016

Copyright © 2017 by Cavendish Square Publishing, LLC

First Edition

Library of Congress Cataloging-in-Publication Data
Names: Byers, Ann, author.
Title: Life as a Native American on the Trail of Tears / Ann Byers.
Description: New York : Cavendish Square Publishing, [2016] | Series: Life as... | Includes index. | Description based on
print version record and CIP data provided by publisher; resource not viewed.
Identifiers: LCCN 2015045779 (print) | LCCN 2015045741 (ebook) | ISBN 9781502617712 (ebook) | ISBN
9781502617941 (pbk.) | ISBN 9781502617835 (library bound) | ISBN 9781502617644 (6 pack)
Subjects: LCSH: Trail of Tears, 1838-1839—Juvenile literature. | Cherokee Indians—Relocation—Juvenile literature. |
Cherokee Indians—History—Juvenile literature.
Classification: LCC E99.C5 (print) | LCC E99.C5 B939 2016 (ebook) | DDC 975.004/97557—dc23
LC record available at http://lccn.loc.gov/2015045779

Editorial Director: David McNamara
Editor: Kristen Susienka
Copy Editor: Rebecca Rohan
Art Director: Jeffrey Talbot
Designer: Alan Sliwinski
Senior Production Manager: Jennifer Ryder-Talbot
Photo Research: J8 Media

The photographs in this book are used by permission and through the courtesy of: National GeographicImage Collection/Alamy Stock Photo, cover and back cover; Linda Moon/Shutterstock.com, 5; North Wind Picture Archives/The Image Works, 6; Public Domain/File:Dahlonega-Mint-1877.jpg/Wikimedia Commons, 9; Matthew Brady/NARA/File:-Gen. Stand Watie - NARA - 529026.jpg/Wikimedia Commons, 10; FPG/Getty Images, 11; Troy Anderson/Native Stock, 14; Matthew Brady/Library of Congress/File:Winfield Scott 1849.jpg/Wikimedia Commons, 16; John Elk/Lonely Plante Images/Getty Images, 19, 24; Thomas R Machnitzki (thomas machnitzki.com)/File:Big Ben Trail Village Creek State Park Wynne AR 2013-09-09 037.jpg/Wikimedia Commons, 20; National Park Service, 22; Marilyn Angel Wynn/Native Stock/ Getty Images, 27.

Printed in the United States of America

Contents

Introduction

Native Americans lived in America for many years. They built houses, had families, and practiced their own religion. But all of that changed in the 1700s and 1800s, when many **settlers** from Europe came to live in America. They built houses where the Native Americans lived. Over the years, more people came. They took land away from Native Americans.

In 1830, President Andrew Jackson said all Native Americans had to move across the river. Some went, but many refused. The president sent soldiers to force them to go. It was a very hard, very sad, 1000-mile (1600-kilometer) trip. Today, this journey is called the Trail of Tears.

The beautiful Great Smoky Mountains were part of Native American land.

A painting of a Native American village in North Carolina made in 1585.

Chapter 1
Natives and Settlers

For hundreds of years, the Native people living in the southeastern United States were hunters and warriors. After the settlers came, the Native American **tribes** began to live more like them. They learned new languages, new traditions, and new religions. Because of this, the settlers called them the Five Civilized Tribes. They were the Cherokees, Creeks, Choctaws, Chickasaws, and Seminoles.

Even though the Native Americans were much like their neighbors, some of the settlers wanted them to leave. The Native Americans lived on lots of land. The settlers wanted to own the land and build on it. They did not want the Native people living there.

A Growing Country

The first Europeans in America settled on the Atlantic coast. As the population grew, people moved westward. In 1803, the US bought the Louisiana Territory, a large area west of the Mississippi, from France. It doubled the size of the United States. People called part of that territory the "Great American Desert." Many people wanted to move there.

Cotton was one reason land was so important there. In 1800, farmers who grew cotton could make a lot of money. But they needed a lot of land to grow the cotton. Another reason was gold. America's first gold rush started in 1828, when gold was discovered in Georgia on Cherokee land. These events brought settlers to Native land and made them want to own the land.

The Dahlonega Mint in Georgia made gold coins during the Georgia gold rush.

When the United States began, each Native American tribe was an independent nation. US citizens did not have rights to land that belonged to any of the tribes. When George Washington was president, the government made promises called treaties that divided the land between the United States and each tribe. The United States promised the Native Americans they could keep their land forever.

Before long, that promise was broken. Settlers wanted the land, and the US government made new treaties with the Native Americans. These treaties paid the tribes for their land. Many tribes lost all of their land. Soon, they were forced to leave their homes.

Stand Watie was one of the Cherokees who signed the Treaty of New Echota.

Chapter 2

Laws and Treaties

Problems started before the new treaties were made. First, leaders in Georgia, where most of the Cherokees lived, gave away land that belonged to Native Americans—including their houses! They asked the US government to move the Native Americans out of the state.

The Cherokees went to court and wrote letters to the president. But President Andrew Jackson

This is an official portrait of President Andrew Jackson.

believed the settlers were right. In 1830, he signed the Indian Removal Act. This law let the president take land from Native Americans in return for other land and money. The other land was west of the Mississippi River, in what is now Oklahoma. It was called "Indian Territory." Jackson wanted all Native people to live in this small area.

Andrew Jackson

Before becoming president, Andrew Jackson was a military general. When he fought a group of Creeks, other tribes helped him. A Cherokee warrior probably saved Jackson's life at the Battle of Horseshoe Bend in 1812. After that battle, Jackson forced the Creeks to sign a peace treaty giving up 23 million acres (9.3 million hectares) of their land.

A few Cherokees thought the deal the president offered was the best option. This small group signed the Treaty of New Echota, giving up all Cherokee land in exchange for land in Oklahoma. The group did not legally speak for the tribe, but the president said the treaty was **valid**. Sixteen thousand Cherokees protested, but Andrew Jackson insisted the Cherokees be removed.

Stages of Removal

After the 1816 treaty ending the Creek War, four thousand Cherokees moved across the Mississippi River into Arkansas. Another two thousand moved west in 1835 when the Treaty of New Echota was signed. When the forced removal started in 1838, a thousand hid in the hills. That left sixteen thousand to walk the Trail of Tears.

This painting by a Cherokee artist portrays Natives on the land route in winter.

Chapter 3
The Journey Begins

All five "civilized tribes" were forced to move to Indian Territory. All five suffered along the way. The Cherokee tribe was the largest of the five tribes. Their experience is called the Trail of Tears.

In May 1838, seven thousand soldiers came to Cherokee land to begin the removal. General Winfield Scott was in charge. Soldiers had built forts in North Carolina, Georgia, Alabama, and Tennessee. The soldiers forced the Natives into the forts. Scott told his men to treat the people kindly.

But many soldiers were harsh. They dragged people out of their homes, poking them with **bayonets**. Family members were separated. Many were not given time

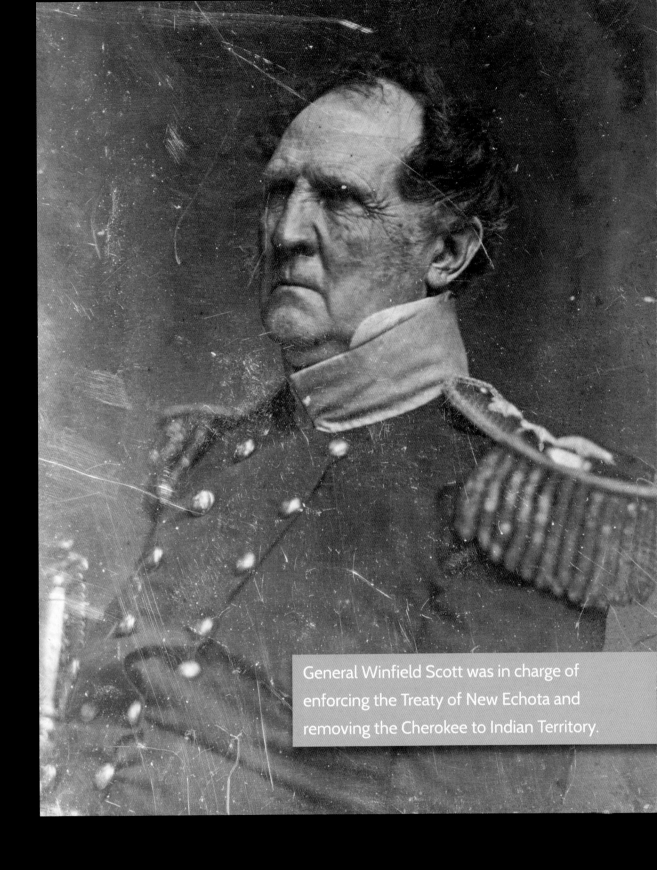

General Winfield Scott was in charge of enforcing the Treaty of New Echota and removing the Cherokee to Indian Territory.

to pack anything. They were barely gone before settlers took over their houses and possessions.

The Native Americans were prisoners while General Scott organized them into sixteen groups for traveling. They did not have enough food, water, or bedding. The forts were dirty and crowded, so diseases spread. Hundreds died there.

By June, General Scott had organized the first three groups to go on the journey. In total, there were about 2,800 Cherokees. He sent them west, each with an army officer and two doctors. They went by boat most of the way on four different rivers and then rode in wagons or walked. This was the "water route." Extremely hot weather and a severe **drought** made travel miserable. Some of the rivers did not have enough water to keep the boats afloat.

General Scott waited for rain and cooler weather before sending the rest of the people. He let the Cherokee chief John Ross decide when to leave, but

Traveling the Trail of Tears

The Trail of Tears saw many men, women, and children walk or ride long distances. These are the states that the Cherokees and other Native Americans traveled through to get to Oklahoma:

Alabama	Kentucky
Arkansas	Missouri
Georgia	North Carolina
Illinois	Tennessee

he had waited too long. The thirteen remaining groups left between October, November, and December. By then, winter was upon them. Travel was worse than miserable; it was deadly. These groups could not use the frozen rivers. The journey, which took two weeks by water, now took up to eight months by land.

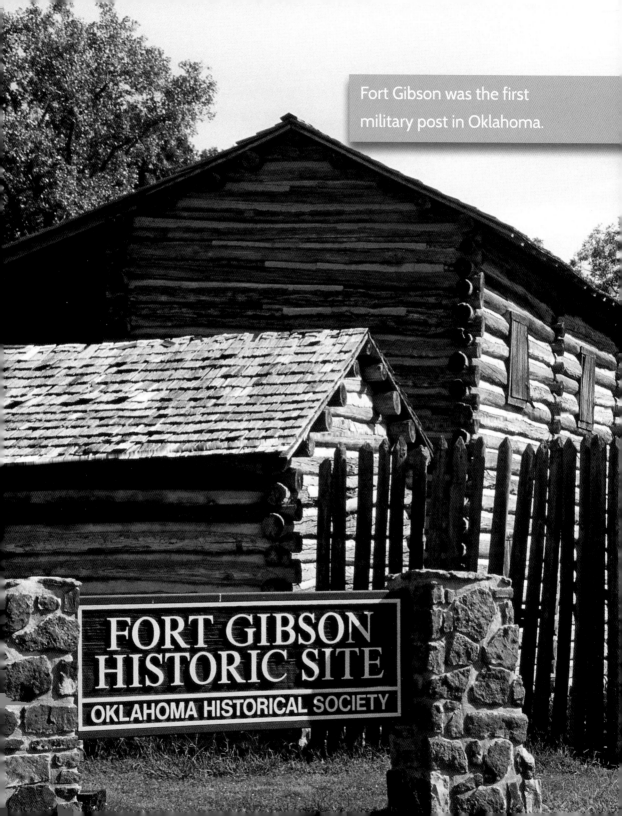

Fort Gibson was the first military post in Oklahoma.

FORT GIBSON
HISTORIC SITE
OKLAHOMA HISTORICAL SOCIETY

This part of the Trail of Tears in Arkansas used to be a military road.

Chapter 4

The Trail Where They Cried

There wasn't just one route from the Native American homelands to Indian Territory. There were actually about ten different trails. The experiences on all the overland routes were the same: hunger, hardship, disease, and death. The Cherokees called this journey "The Trail Where They Cried."

Because the last groups of people left later than planned, much of the food set aside for the journey was used up before the trip started. General Scott thought they could find food along the way. But the summer's drought meant trees and fields were bare. There was not enough grass for the horses and oxen. There were fewer than usual deer, squirrels, and other

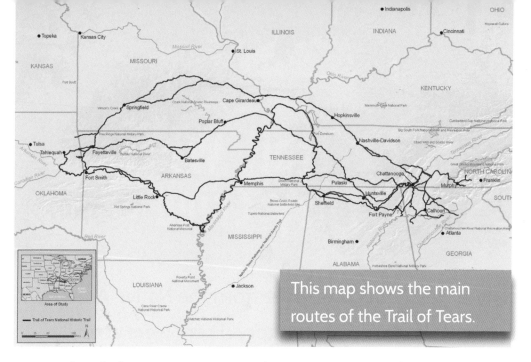

This map shows the main routes of the Trail of Tears.

animals. If the group passed near a town, the leader could try to buy food. But there were not many towns, prices were high, and money was scarce.

Much of the route was wilderness. The stronger Cherokees cut paths through the trees so wagons could fit. When the rains finally came, the dirt turned to mud. The streams and creeks overflowed, and many people drowned trying to cross them.

The worst part came with the winter snow. Many of the Cherokees had no shoes and no blankets. They slept in wagons or on the frozen ground, often

Supplies

For the removal, the US government provided six hundred wagons and carts, five thousand horses, and one hundred oxen. The wagons had room for only the old, the young, and the sick. The government provided corn, flour, coffee, sugar, and a little salt pork. The food was not very good, and it was not enough. Doctors went with each group, but they did not have enough medicine. The government did not provide blankets or warm clothing.

without a campfire. Families huddled together for warmth, passing diseases from one to another. Every day people died from sickness, hunger, or exhaustion. They were buried along the way in shallow, unmarked graves because the ground was frozen, and the group had to keep moving.

Reconstruction of the first Cherokee Council House built in Oklahoma.

Chapter 5

A New Beginning

Of the sixteen thousand Cherokees forced to move west, over four thousand died on the trail. Hundreds more died in the forts before the journey began. Those who survived made new lives in Oklahoma. They faced many challenges, including disagreements with the Cherokees who were already in the new territory. Slowly they built homes, schools, churches, and businesses.

Before long, settlers began moving into Indian Territory. To make room for them, the US government broke its promises to the Native Americans. When Oklahoma became a state in 1907, Indian Territory and its people became part of the new state.

But the Cherokees kept working for their independence. Many men and women worked hard to help the Cherokee Nation become what it is today. Eventually, their hard work paid off.

Today, the US government officially recognizes the Cherokee Nation as a **sovereign** nation. This means the Cherokees are citizens of both the Cherokee Nation and the United States. The Cherokees do not live on a reservation, like some Native American tribes do. They make their own laws and have their own police and schools. They also have their own government. The capital of the Cherokee Nation is in Tahlequah, Oklahoma. Many schools teach the Cherokee language and English to their students. Every year, the Cherokees celebrate their history with dances and ceremonies. They are a proud nation with a long history and a bright future.

This sign at the Cherokee Nation's headquarters says "Cherokee Nation" in Cherokee and English.

Glossary

bayonet A pointed blade attached to the end of a rifle or other long gun.

drought A period of time without enough rain for plants to grow well.

settler A person who builds a home in a different area of the world.

sovereign Independent, with the right to govern itself.

tribe A group of Native Americans that believes the same things and lives together.

valid Good, legal.

Find Out More

Books

Bruchac, Joseph. *On This Long Journey: The Journal of Jesse Smoke, a Cherokee Boy, the Trail of Tears, 1838*. Steelville, MO: Sanval, 2014.

Jones, Veda Boyd. *Nellie the Brave: The Cherokee Trail of Tears*. Uhrichsville, OH: Barbour, 2013.

Peppas, Lynn. *Trail of Tears*. New York: Crabtree, 2013.

Website

Cherokee Tribe Information for Kids

www.warpaths2peacepipes.com/indian-tribes/cherokee-tribe.htm

Video

Trail of Tears

vimeo.com/93161013

Index

Page numbers in **boldface** are illustrations. Entries in **boldface** are glossary terms.

About the Author

Ann Byers is a teacher and youth worker. She lived and taught school on the Navajo reservation in Kaibeto, Arizona. She wrote *The Trail of Tears: A Primary Source History of the Forced Relocation of the Cherokee Nation*. She currently lives in California.